Know God
Published by Orange, a division of The reThink Group, Inc.
5870 Charlotte Lane, Suite 300
Cumming, GA 30040 U.S.A.

The Orange logo is a registered trademark of The reThink Group, Inc.

All Scripture quotations, unless otherwise noted, are taken from the *Holy Bible, New
International Version®. NIV®.* Copyright © 1973, 1978, 1984 by International Bible
Society. Used by permission of Zondervan.

Other Orange products are available online and direct from the publisher. Visit our
website at www.WhatIsOrange.org for more resources like these.

ISBN: 978-1-941259-74-0

©2016 The reThink Group, Inc.

reThink Conceptual Team:
Ben Crawshaw, Kristen Ivy, Reggie Joiner, Cara Martens, Dan Scott
Lead Writer: Ben Crawshaw
Editing Team: Lauren Makahon, Mike Jeffries, Lauren Terrell, Jennifer Wilder, Sam Collier
Art Direction: Ryan Boon
Project Manager: Nate Brandt
Design: FiveStone

Printed in the United States of America
Second Edition 2016

5 6 7 8 9 10 11 12 13 14

06/09/2022

# KNOW GOD

# DON'T READ THIS BOOK

**DON'T READ THIS BOOK.**

**Wait, wait. That came out wrong. Of course I want you to read it. But don't *just* read this book.**

Write in it. Draw on it. Mark it up.

If you've never written in a book, today's a perfect day to start.

If you're not a write-in-your-book kind of person, don't sweat it.

Text yourself instead.

AND

Find someone else to text and talk to about this book.

Think of one person you know who loves God.
Make sure it's someone you feel comfortable talking to.

Your dad? Mentor? Small group leader? Student pastor? Dentist?

You choose.

Okay. Got someone in mind?

Good. Now, I'm going to tell you the most important thing you will do with this book.

## TEAR OUT THIS PAGE ⟶
and give it to that person.

Because I want them to go on this journey with you. It'll be better than just thinking about these things alone.

What's up?

I just got a journal called *Know God.* I wanted to tell you about it because you seem like you know God. And even though this is a pretty cool book, it won't be able to tell me everything I need to know about knowing God. So when I handed you this page, it was my way of asking you if we can talk through this together.

So . . . can you help me out?

This journal has **short readings** for 28 days. That's four weeks. I'm not sure I'll be able to do every single day, but I'm going to give it my best shot. Do you think you can encourage me stick with it? And if I get off track, can you challenge me to get back on?

Yes? No? Maybe?

One more thing: At the end of each week, can we get together and talk through what I'm learning? I might have some questions. And I believe you'll have some questions for me, too. (That was a hint; there are some questions on the back of this page that might be helpful to ask when we get together.)

I really appreciate your influence in my life. I'm excited about the next four weeks. Thanks for walking through them with me.

Sincerely,

Thanks for hanging out with me for the next four weeks. Any time we get together, feel free to ask me things like: What's the most interesting thing you read this week? Was there something that you had a question about?

But more specifically, here's what I'll be learning. Let's start by talking about this:

## WEEK ONE

This week I discovered that in order to know God, I need to **HEAR** from God.

I LEARNED THAT:

» Creation points to the Creator.
» Jesus' words reveal God's heart.
» The Bible is God's Word.
» The Bible gives our lives direction.
» Reading the Bible is a good habit.
» Memorizing Scripture changes us.
» The Holy Spirit is God's stamp of ownership.

When we get together this week, ask me if I have a plan for reading God's Word. Maybe we could even come up with one together.

## WEEK TWO

This week I discovered that in order to know God, I need to **PRAY** to God.

I LEARNED THAT:

» Prayer helps us get to know God.
» God loves authentic prayers.
» Prayer reminds us who God is.
» God moves when we ask Him to take the lead.
» Prayer reminds us that we need God.
» God forgave us so we should forgive others.
» I have access to God—any time, any place.

When we get together this week, ask me about my prayers. Maybe you could even share one thing you have discovered about prayer in your own life.

## WEEK THREE

This week I discovered that in order to know God, I need to **TALK** about God.

I LEARNED THAT:

» We all need support from good friends.
» I should talk about who Jesus is.
» I can cheer on others in their faith.
» God reveals Himself through our questions.
» Remembering what God has done builds our faith.
» I don't have to know everything in order to share what I do know.
» I am created to be a light in the dark.

When we get together this week, ask me when—and with whom—I am talking about my relationship with God (other than "right now" and "with you").

## WEEK FOUR

This week I discovered that in order to know God, I need to **LIVE** a life that honors God.

I LEARNED THAT:

» God is worth our worship.
» God's love is free.
» God loves it when we give generously.
» The way to find my life is to give it away.
» My work is an act of worship.
» When I trust God, I will rest.
» I should start with love.

When we get together this week, ask me how I am worshiping God in the way I live. Maybe we can think of some new ways we could both give, serve, and love others.

KNOWING GOD IS A
LOT LIKE KNOWING ANYONE
ELSE—YOU CAN LEARN A
LOT ABOUT THEM, BUT THEY
STILL SURPRISE YOU EVERY
NOW AND THEN.

# HOW DO I KNOW GOD?

Knowing God doesn't happen in a moment. It's not like you wake up one morning and *BAM*, you know God. You have Him all figured out—everything there is to know. No more questions or doubts.

It doesn't work like that.

In fact, I bet if you talked to people who believe in God and have known Him for a long time, 100% of them would tell you they're still discovering new things about Him. They still have questions. God is still mysterious to them.

Go ahead. Ask them. See what they say.

Knowing God is a lot like knowing anyone else—
You can learn a lot about them, but they still surprise you every now and then. They aren't puzzles to be solved. Or textbooks to be read.
They're *people* to hang out with.

Knowing God is the same way.
Knowing God is about a RELATIONSHIP.

You can read every word in this book, fill in every blank, follow every suggestion, and still not understand all there is to know about God.

And that's okay. Because this book isn't about knowing everything there is to know about God. It's about a journey. A journey where you will . . .

Learn new things.
Unlearn what you thought you knew.
Connect with a God who already loves you more than you will ever know.

But before you go any further—
Before you even turn to the next page—
There is one thing you absolutely must know about knowing God:

**If you want to know God, start with Jesus.**

I realize that's a pretty predictable thing to say. But really, Jesus is the place to start. Why? Well, because Jesus *is* God. But Jesus was also a Man.
He was born.
He had a mother.

She gave Him chores and a curfew. (I have no idea if He had a curfew.)

He had birthdays. I don't know how He celebrated them, but He had them.

He . . .
. . . ate.
. . . slept.
. . . got thirsty.
. . . sneezed.
I could go on and on.

Jesus was literally God walking around on earth like you and me. So what Jesus *said*—yeah, those are God's words. And what He *did*—well, that should give us a pretty good idea of what God is like.

**So, if you really want to know God, get to know Jesus.**

# HOW DO I KNOW JESUS?

I guess that's the next logical question, right? I mean, Jesus isn't exactly sending you texts, retweeting you, or sharing pics on Instagram. Although, if He did, that would make for an awesome story.

So how do we get to know Him?

**If you want to know Jesus, read His Story.**

Jesus' story is the Bible. Maybe you have a Bible that your grandma gave you seven years ago. Or maybe you have a fancy app that lets you search funny verses about donkeys. But let's be honest—other than settling an argument or answering a question at church, how much have you interacted with the Bible?

You may not know this, but the Bible is not a book. I thought it was a book for most of my life. I mean, it looks like a book. You can flip through it like a book. You can download it like a book.

But it's really not one book. It's 66 books written by 40 authors over 1,600 years.

And it all comes together to tell ONE STORY.

It's not just any story. It's a story about:
A really big God who loved sinful people SO MUCH
He became a human.

Jesus.

And Jesus
lived,
died,
and rose again
so we could be forgiven and live with Him forever.

**This is the story that helps us know Jesus.**
**This is the story that gives us a background for everything we know about God.**

**⊘ HERE ARE A FEW THINGS WE KNOW ABOUT GOD BECAUSE OF HIS STORY:**

» We know God is good because He created a perfect world.

» We know bad things will happen because when people went against God, the world became broken.

» We know God won't abandon us because we see how He pursued sinful and disobedient people for thousands of years.

» We know we can trust God to keep His promises because He already kept His greatest promise by sending His Son.

» We know we can be forgiven because Jesus died for us and already took on all the punishment for our sin.

» We know that one day we can live with God in Heaven because Jesus defeated death once and for all.

» We know that until we see God face-to-face, we are called to live a life that is characterized by love because that's what Jesus taught.

# THE BIG IDEA.

Are you tracking with me so far? Let's review.
You want to know God? Great!
Start by getting to know Jesus.
The best way to know Jesus is to read His story—the Bible. Specifically, the part where He shows up on the scene.

In other words, start by reading the Gospels (Matthew, Mark, Luke, John). Four different accounts written by four different men.
All about what Jesus said and did.

But even before you read the Gospels, you might be interested to know there is one thing Jesus *did* that is more important than anything else.

You can probably guess what it is. He died for the sins of the world, and after three days, He rose from the dead—not like some-zombie-in-a-video-game alive again, but like walking-around-eating-breakfast-with-His-friends alive again.

Jesus died. He rose to life again. He's alive. And that's the most important thing He did.

But there was also something important that Jesus *said*.
Okay, *everything* He said was important. *Really important.*
But there was one thing He said that was more important than anything else.
Not according to me. According to Him.
Of all the things Jesus said, this one thing is the key to understanding everything you'll ever know about God.

Jesus said this one thing on a day when a group of religious leaders—men who had spent their entire lives studying God—approached Him. One of them asked Him this question:

*"Teacher, what is the most important commandment in the law?"*

Check out what Jesus said:

*"'Love the Lord your God with all your heart and with all your soul and with all your mind.' This is the first and greatest commandment. And the second is like it: 'Love your neighbor as yourself.' All the Law and the Prophets hang on these two commandments" (Matthew 22: 37-40).*

That's it.

**The most important commandment.**
**The biggest idea.**
Everything else that the Bible teaches comes back to this.
If you start to understand these 48 words now,
you can worry about the other hundreds of thousands of words in the Bible later.

Because really, it's pretty simple.
The most important thing you could ever do is **LOVE GOD**.

And if you aren't sure how to love God, a good way to start is by loving the people He loves:
God loves *you*.
And God loves *others*.

You can know for sure that God loves *you* because He created you. And He cared enough about you to show up on this planet to die for you so you can be forgiven and be with Him forever.

And you can know for certain that God loves *others* because, guess what, He created them and died for them, too. All of them. The people you'd give your last stick of gum to and the people who make you want to move to the South Pole.

It's like Jesus summed up everything you need to know by saying: *It's about three relationships: God. You. Others.*

OR IF YOU WANT TO MAKE IT MORE SIMPLE, IT'S ABOUT ONE IDEA:

# LOVE.

Love God.
See yourself the way He sees you (with amazing love).
Love others the way He loves them.

That's where Jesus started. So as you begin this journey, I think it makes sense for you to start there, too.

# TO SUM IT ALL UP

**1**

When you get
to know
**GOD'S STORY**
it helps you
understand your own
story. (You know more
about yourself because
you understand more
about the One who
made you).

**2**

Then as you
understand
**YOUR STORY**
it helps you see how
you're connected to
the stories of others.

**3**

So, the way to
begin living out
**OUR STORY**
is to love others
the way that God
loves them.

SEE HOW THAT WORKS?

# 4 WAYS TO KNOW GOD

EVEN THOUGH THERE'S NO FORMULA FOR KNOWING EVERYTHING ABOUT GOD, THERE ARE A FEW THINGS YOU CAN DO EVERY DAY THAT WILL HELP YOU KNOW HIM BETTER.

## HEAR

If you want to know someone, what's one of the first things you do? You listen. Guys, good luck getting a girl to agree to a 2nd date if you don't listen to what she says. Girls, if you're dating a guy who never listens to you, stop! Why is listening so important? Because *that other person* is the only one who can tell you what he or she is thinking and feeling, and what makes him or her laugh or get angry. The same is true for God. If you want to know God, you have to learn how to listen. And when you get in the habit of hearing from Him, it helps you *trust* Him more.

## PRAY

Have you ever been in a relationship where the other person did ALL the talking? That's weird, right? God thinks so, too. He doesn't want a relationship with you where He's the only one talking. Sure, He has moments where He just wants you to be quiet and listen. But for the most part, He wants you to talk back. He wants to hear from you—your frustrations, worries, fears, dreams, requests, and interests. So if you want to know God, get in the habit of talking with Him. Because when you pray, it *connects* you with God.

THAT'S WHAT THIS JOURNAL IS ALL ABOUT—FOUR THINGS THAT YOU CAN DO TODAY (AND EVERY DAY) THAT WILL HELP YOU **KNOW GOD**.

# TALK

Who is your closest friend? Do you talk about that person when he's not around? Sure you do. Not in a bad, trash-talking kind of way. In a good way. You talk about the back flip he did off a brick wall. You talk about the hilarious joke he told. You talk about where you hung out this weekend. In fact, you probably hang out with people who also like hanging out with your friend. The same is true with God. As you get to know Him, you'll find that you want to talk about Him more. You want to be around other people who talk about Him. And when you talk about Him—and listen to others talk about Him—it helps you *see* Him in new ways.

# LIVE

Have you ever had someone give you a gift or do something for you that was ridiculously nice? Like, so unbelievably amazing that you just *had* to find a way to thank them? The same is true with God. As you get to know God more, you will discover more and more about how awesome He is. Don't be surprised if you find yourself wanting to say *thank you* in your own unique way. Maybe you'll respond by singing, jumping up and down, silently thinking about Him, painting a picture, serving the homeless, or volunteering to help kids at your church. Regardless of how you do it, the more time you spend with God, the more you will want to respond to His greatness by *honoring* God with your life.

Summary of last weeks from kids
here before

How has this looked since we
started

Any questions before we start this
week?

# HEAR

# HEAR

If you want to know God, the first thing you want to do is hear from Him. But how do you hear from Someone who isn't likely to . . .

. . . walk onto your school campus.
. . . sit next to you at lunch.
. . . send you a text.
. . . or hang out with you on a Friday night?

How can you hear from Someone if you can't even see Him? Actually, the Bible gives us a pretty good clue. It says this:

[ **"No one has ever seen God, but God the One and Only, who is at the Father's side, has made him known" (John 1:18).** ]

The One and Only who is at the Father's side. That's Jesus. There it is again— this idea that **if you want to** know God, **get to know Jesus.** Jesus is the best way to know God because Jesus walked around on this planet and *showed us what God is like.* He's not physically here now, but He was here. And while He was here, He spent a lot of time with 12 guys who are sometimes called [*disciples*] and sometimes called [*apostles.*] Call them whatever you want. The point is, they got to know Jesus pretty well.

*we know how Jesus knows people through how He treats disciples*

They were there when Jesus taught.
They were there when Jesus did some incredible miracles.
They were there when Jesus died,
And all of them (except Judas) were there to see Him alive once again after He rose from the dead.

They were also around when Jesus ascended into Heaven after rising from the dead. Meaning, one minute He's chillin' on a hill outside Jerusalem, and the next minute He's floating up into the sky until He disappears. (At least, that's how I picture it in my head.)
Check out Acts 1 to see for yourself.

So why does it matter that these guys witnessed so much of Jesus' life and ministry? And what does that have to do with hearing from God? A lot.

Right before Jesus ascended, He gave them the most important mission: Go. Tell people what you've seen and heard.

> **"You will be my witnesses in Jerusalem, and in all Judea and Samaria, and to the ends of the earth" (Acts 1:8).**

And guess what? They did.

They went. They told. Some of them even wrote about it.

Two of Jesus' disciples wrote down everything they knew about Him. Think about it—these guys knew Jesus. He was their friend, wingman, bro, amigo, bff (okay, I'll stop now). When they wrote about Jesus, they were writing about Someone they had traveled with, eaten with, camped with, and hung out with. They had seen Him in action.

They wrote about His birth. They wrote about how His ministry got started. They put down on paper everything they could remember about what He did and said. You might recognize their names: Matthew and John.

Then there were Mark and Luke. Mark and Luke weren't in the group of 12 guys who hung out with Jesus, but they knew some of those guys. Mark was friends with Peter, and Luke interviewed just about everybody who had an experience with Jesus. And these two guys also wrote about Jesus based on eyewitness accounts.

Today you can still read the words of Matthew, Mark, Luke and John. They're the first four books of the New Testament. We call them the Gospels, and each one gives us an interesting point of view on the life of Jesus.

If you want to know God, read His story. Think about who He is and what He says. Hearing from God in this way will help you trust Him

So here's one thing to think about as you start this week:
**If you want to Know God, remember His words.**

# HEAR

## DAY 1

Did you know that 45,000 thunderstorms occur every day? Sounds almost impossible, right? It also makes me want to take a nap. Because what's better than a nap during a thunderstorm? No, seriously. What's better?

Wait! Wake up! No napping—even if there is a thunderstorm where you are. And listen to this: According to the space agency NASA, you'd have to explode *100 billion tons* of dynamite *every second* to match the energy produced by the sun. That's insane to think about!

Whether it's clouds, rain, lightning, stars, the sun, the moon, or the expanse of the sky, if you go outside and look *up,* there's a lot going on. But very few of us—myself included—spend much time looking that direction. (Probably because I'm looking down at my phone too much.)

King David, one of the most famous kings of Israel, wrote about *looking up* as a way to know God. There's a book in the Old Testament called *Psalms,* which means *praise songs.* David wrote several songs. And although you won't hear one of David's psalms on Spotify or iTunes, you can still appreciate it as good music. Check out this lyric:

> **"The heavens declare the glory of God; the skies proclaim the work of His hands" (Psalm 19:1).**

**❂ WHAT DO YOU THINK THIS VERSE MEANS?**

......................................................................................................

......................................................................................................

......................................................................................................

Nature *declares* and *proclaims.* **Creation points to the Creator.** Nature says something. It makes an announcement. The question is, do we hear what nature is saying?

# HEAR

David believed nature made statements about God. Statements like:

*God is an astounding Creator.*
*God's creativity is unending.*
*The beauty around us reflects God's glory. (Glory = Honor + Awe)*

Jesus had a similar thought:

**"Look at the birds of the air; they do not sow or reap or store away in barns, and yet your heavenly Father feeds them. Are you not much more valuable than they?" (Matthew 6:26).**

Jesus urges us to open our eyes to what's around us. Because by paying attention to *creation*, we can better understand our *Creator*. Even more, we can catch a glimpse of the great love our Creator has for us.

With that in mind, here's a two-part challenge for today:

1. **Look around.** Go outside. Take a walk. Pay attention to creation. Ask yourself, what does *this* say about its Creator?

2. **Say thanks.** Tell God you appreciate His work. Maybe something like this: *God, thank You for the creativity You put into nature. I know that all creation points back to You. So in seeing this, I appreciate You more.*

Nature makes an announcement about God. The question is *are we listening?* It's time for us to hear God and know God.

**❍ AFTER SPENDING SOME TIME OUTSIDE, WHAT DID YOU LEARN ABOUT GOD?**

.................................................................................................................

.................................................................................................................

.................................................................................................................

# HEAR

## —— DAY 2 ——

Before Jesus became famous for being, well, Jesus, He had a job. And I'm not talking about being Savior of the world—though He was certainly that. But for a period of time, Jesus had an actual trade job.

Now there's a lot of conversations about exactly which job He had. From what I've seen, the argument comes down to four professional titles that Jesus possibly held:

1. Carpenter

2. Mason

3. Engineer

4. Handyman

So which is the correct answer? I have no idea. But one thing we can be sure of is that Jesus was in the construction business—which makes sense because he told a story about building a house.

But before we get to that story, consider what it means to follow God. Does your mind immediately go to *rules*? You know, all the stuff you should and shouldn't do? All the people you should avoid hanging out with? Or maybe the ones you should be nice to, forgive, encourage, help and love?

**◐ TAKE A MINUTE TO NAME SOME THINGS YOU THINK GOD WANTS YOU TO DO OR NOT DO:**

......................................................................................................

......................................................................................................

......................................................................................................

# HEAR

Here's another question: Why *should* you do (or not do) these things? With Jesus' experience with construction on your mind, listen to this excerpt. It will help us answer that question:

> *"Therefore everyone who hears these words of mine and puts them into practice is like a wise man who built his house on the rock. . . . But everyone who hears these words of mine and does not put them into practice is like a foolish man who built his house on sand"* (Matthew 7:24, 26).

Jesus goes on to say that a storm came. The house on the rock took it like a champ. The house on the sand? Crumbled. Destroyed. Woodpile for a bonfire or a fireplace.

Jesus' story tells us:

1. **What we should do.** He makes it as obvious as possible—build your life on Jesus' words. Put them into practice.

2. **Why we should do it.** Not just because our parents, pastors or church leaders say so, but because it's smart. This isn't about a list of rules—this is about building something that won't break.

**Jesus' words reveal God's heart**. When you study the words of Jesus, it will help you know God more. But Jesus' words won't really do much until you apply them. When the storms come, you'll be happy you built your homes (lives) on the rock (Jesus' words). It won't keep the storms from happening, but it will make us better prepared to handle them.

**◑ WHAT DO YOU WANT TO BUILD YOUR LIFE ON? HOW DO YOU PLAN ON DOING THAT?**

.......................................................................................................................

.......................................................................................................................

.......................................................................................................................

# HEAR

## —————— DAY 3 ——————

Do you yawn a lot? (Are you yawning right now?) Although there are lots of thoughts about *why* we yawn, none of them have been proven. The ancient Greeks believed that yawning was a person's soul trying to escape his or her body. If that's the case, my soul has probably made it to the other side of the world and back by now.

Another theory is that *boredom* is the cause. If I'm having a conversation with someone and he starts yawning, I assume he'd rather be reading the iTunes' terms of service agreement.

If boredom is, in fact, the cause of yawning, let me ask you a question: Does the idea of reading the Bible automatically make you yawn? I've had conversations with students who think they *should* read the Bible, but they don't because it's boring. Or old. Or hard to understand.

I'll be honest, there are some parts of the Bible that are less than riveting— like instructions on burnt offerings or measurements of the temple. I just typed the names of those things and yawned. Twice.

**❸ TALK ABOUT YOUR HISTORY WITH THE BIBLE. HAVE YOU READ IT A LOT? A LITTLE? NEVER? WHAT DO YOU THINK ABOUT THE BIBLE?**

........................................................................................................................

........................................................................................................................

........................................................................................................................

Here's another question: Do you think the Bible is relevant to your life *right now*? Do you believe it has something to say about your family, friends, dating life, grades, etc.?

# HEAR

In the New Testament, there is a letter written by Paul to one of his best friends, Timothy. And in that letter, Paul talks about the idea of Scripture being *alive:*

> *"All scripture is God-breathed and is useful for teaching, rebuking, correcting and training in righteousness, so that the man of God may be thoroughly equipped for every good work" (2 Timothy 3:16-17).*

Paul makes two definitive statements in this verse:

1. **All Scripture is *God-breathed.*** It is inspired by God. It's not just words *about* God—the Bible *is* God's words.

2. **All Scripture is *useful.*** The Bible helps us *know* what is right. But it also helps us *do* what is right. That's the payoff—that we may be prepared to follow God's words.

Now, that doesn't mean that you'll never be bored reading the Bible. And it certainly doesn't mean you'll understand it all. But you can trust that **the Bible is God's Word.** For you. And those words are *alive.* If you want to know God, listen to His words in the Bible.

## DAY 4

Can you imagine driving a car at night without turning the headlights on? Maybe that sounds cool to you because you're into life-threatening experiences that are likely to get your car totaled. But to me? That sounds like a nightmare.

It's true: things are just easier when they're done in the light.
Do ever feel like you're navigating *life* in the dark? You're not sure which way you're supposed to go? You have situations where you wish the answers were clearer?

**◐ WHAT ARE SOME AREAS IN YOUR LIFE WHERE MAYBE YOU FEEL LIKE YOU'RE DRIVING IN THE DARK AND YOU WISH YOU COULD GET A LITTLE LIGHT?**

........................................................................................................

........................................................................................................

........................................................................................................

The Bible tells us what "light" we need to illuminate the dark areas of life:

> *"Your word is a lamp to my feet a light for my path"*
> *(Psalm 119:105).*

If you were hiking on a trail at night and wanted to avoid falling off a cliff, you would hold up a light. Why? So you knew where you were supposed to go. That's what the Bible does—it gives us information so we can see clearly. In other words, **the Bible gives our lives direction.**

Psalm 119 is the longest chapter in the Bible and it's all about God's Word. In fact, the author of the psalm refers to God's Word in almost all 176 verses. And the entire chapter is about how God's words help us stay on track with what God wants for us. The goal of the chapter? That we would know God better as we allow His words to guide our lives.

**◑ IF YOU WANT TO START READING YOUR BIBLE, BUT YOU AREN'T SURE HOW TO BEGIN, HERE ARE TWO SUGGESTIONS:**

1. **Find a good starting place in your Bible.** Don't play Bible Roulette, where you close your eyes and randomly open your Bible to read it. You wouldn't read a normal book like that (or you shouldn't, anyway). Start at the beginning of a book. Here are some good ones to try:

   John
   Mark
   Proverbs
   Psalms
   Philippians

2. **Have a reading goal.** Growing up, my dad used to tell me, "You don't have to understand *everything*. Just read until you understand *something*." I still put that into practice today. I read until I bump into something that I can relate to. Here are some questions that help me:

   What does this passage say?
   What does this passage tell me about God?
   How does this passage apply to me right now?

When the Bible begins to light up your life, it's exciting! Not only do you begin to know God better, you begin to trust Him more because you see how His words give your life direction.

# HEAR

## DAY 5

Do you have any habits? Do you crack your knuckles? Twirl your hair? Smack your gum? Check your phone every 1.3 seconds? You may need to ask someone who knows you well what your habits are. They may be so habitual that you don't even realize you have them!

The thing about habits is that *bad* ones are a lot easier to establish than *good* ones.

**❷ NAME TWO HABITS THAT YOU HAVE THAT YOU'VE FORMED WITHOUT REALLY THINKING ABOUT THEM. (IN OTHER WORDS, NO ONE TOLD YOU TO DO IT; YOU DIDN'T WAKE UP AND DECIDE ONE DAY YOU WERE GOING TO DO IT.)**

..............................................................................................................

**❷ NAME ONE HABIT THAT YOU HAVE THAT'S ON PURPOSE.**

..............................................................................................................

**Reading the Bible is a good habit**. Why? To answer that question, I'll throw an old saying at you: "First you make your habits, then your habits make you." In other words, reading the Bible will influence who you become.

There are a number of reasons why people don't make reading their Bible a habit:

- » They don't have time.
- » They're not good at it (meaning they don't know where to start, or they don't understand what they read).
- » They don't feel like it.

I'm not so sure I'd call those *reasons*. I'd call them excuses. But what if you quit making excuses?

# HEAR

Just like studying, exercising, saving, or practicing, when you read your Bible regularly, you get something in return. The author of Psalm 1 says it this way:

> *"Blessed is the man who does not walk in the counsel of the wicked. . . . But his delight is in the law of the LORD, and on his law he meditates day and night. He is like a tree planted by streams of water which yields its fruit in season"*
> *(Psalm 1:1-3).*

**◔ WHAT IS THE MAIN POINT OF THIS PASSAGE?**

..................................................................................................................

..................................................................................................................

..................................................................................................................

**◔ HOW DOES THIS PASSAGE APPLY TO YOU RIGHT NOW?**

..................................................................................................................

..................................................................................................................

..................................................................................................................

"Like a tree planted by streams of water," when you're constantly drinking in God's Word, your character is always being changed for the better—you're always bearing fruit at the right time.

This passage isn't referring to people who only read the Bible when they're in trouble or faced with a desperate decision, it's talking about people who make it a lifestyle—who have a long-term goal of knowing God.

Why don't you try it?
1. Pick a consistent time.
2. Pick a consistent place.
3. Make it a habit by committing to 90 days.

# HEAR

## DAY 6

The human brain is an amazing organ. In fact, the brain's memory storage space measures around 2.5 petabytes (or a million gigabytes)! That means your brain can hold more data than 15,500 iPhones. Think of it this way: If your brain worked like a digital video recorder in a television, 2.5 petabytes would be enough to hold three million hours worth of television shows. You'd have to leave the television running continuously for more than 300 years to use up all that storage. I want to see a DVR do that!

**❂ KNOWING THIS, WHY DO YOU THINK IT'S SO CHALLENGING FOR US TO MEMORIZE SCRIPTURE?**

........................................................................................................

........................................................................................................

........................................................................................................

Today I want to challenge you to put that awesome brain to work and replace just a few of those JT lyrics with some Scripture.

You may ask, "But why is it important to memorize Scripture? It's right there in the Bible to read, so why waste precious brain space committing it to memory?" Listen to this:

*"I seek you with all my heart; do not let me stray from your commands. I have hidden your word in my heart that I might not sin against you" (Psalm 119:10-11).*

**Memorizing Scripture changes us.** It transforms our minds. When you have God's words in your brain, you literally hear from God more often. Your thoughts are more focused *towards* God. And as a result, you'll start to know Him better.

Do you know the Pledge of Allegiance?
Do you know your phone number, address and social security number?
Do you know the lyrics to at least one Taylor Swift song?
(Guys, be honest!)

You know these things through repetition. A thought is a physical pathway in the brain. The more you have that thought, the more you groove that path into your mind, and the easier it is to have that thought again. Memorizing Scripture takes work. It takes repetition. But it's possible for every single person who has a brain. (That means you!)

I've given you a whole list of great verses for you to memorize—you'll see it later. But for today, I want you to practice by memorizing *half* of the verse we studied:

> *"I have hidden your word in my heart that I might not sin against you."*

There. You've seen it. Don't let your smart phone be smarter than you. Memorize some Scripture and see what happens.

# HEAR

## DAY 7

According to *ehow.com*, there are six ways to know if you've seen a ghost. Two of those methods include testing electronic appliances and observing the behavior of wild animals in the area. I could probably figure out how to test my appliances. But recording the behavior of wild animals? That sounds scarier than seeing a ghost.

If you're the kind of person who finds ghosts interesting, you should read the Bible. Check this out: When Jesus soared into the sky after coming back from the dead, He sent His Holy Ghost to us. Question: *Do you still think the Bible is boring?* Because that's straight-up mind-blowing (and, I'll admit, a little freaky) to think about.

Have you ever heard the term "Trinity"? It refers to the three distinct Persons of God:

1. **God the Father.** He's the Creator of the whole universe. He created the earth and everything in it. When sin entered the world through Adam and Eve's disobedience to Him, God sent a solution to save His creation. He sent:
2. **God the Son.** Jesus. Jesus lived a perfect life, died, and was later resurrected. But when Jesus ascended into heaven, He sent a Helper to those who believed in Him. He sent:
3. **God the Holy Spirit.** This is who we're talking about today. I grew up hearing Him referred to as the "Holy Ghost." The Holy Spirit is God's presence who lives in followers of Jesus.

**◑ LOTS OF CHRISTIANS THROUGHOUT HISTORY HAVE DEBATED ABOUT HOW TO DISCUSS OR MAKE SENSE OF THE TRINITY. ONE GOD, BUT THREE PERSONS. WHY DON'T YOU TAKE A SHOT AT IT? HOW WOULD YOU DESCRIBE THE TRINITY?**

........................................................................................................

........................................................................................................

........................................................................................................

In 2 Corinthians, the Apostle Paul says this of the Holy Spirit:

> *"[He] put his Spirit in our hearts as a deposit, guaranteeing what is to come" (2 Corinthians 1:22).*

"He" is God.

"Our" includes anyone who believes in Him.

Paul is saying that anyone who believes in God has God's Holy Spirit in their hearts. God's Holy Spirit in us is His way of promising: *"You will be Mine forever. Your life will go up and down. You will have good days and bad. But My Spirit in you is the promise I am always here to help you."*

Weirded out, yet? Totally confused? That's okay. You don't have to understand the Trinity or even the Holy Spirit to experience God's presence. Just start here: **The Holy Spirit is God's stamp of ownership.**

And when you are reading God's Word and tuned in to His Spirit in your life, you will begin to hear from God in new and exciting ways.

Spend a few minutes praying. Ask God to speak to you through His Spirit. Ask for His Holy Spirit to give you strength in any struggle you are currently facing.

## IF YOU WANT TO KNOW GOD . . .
## REMEMBER HIS WORDS.

---

❂ THERE ARE LOTS OF VERSES IN THE BIBLE THAT ARE WORTH REMEMBERING. HERE ARE A FEW TO GET YOU STARTED:

"We are God's workmanship, created in Christ Jesus to do good works, which God prepared in advance for us to do."
   (EPHESIANS 2:10)

"Trust in the LORD with all your heart and lean not on your own understanding; in all your ways acknowledge him, and he will make your paths straight."
   (PROVERBS 3:5-6)

"Neither height nor depth, nor anything else in all creation, will be able to separate us from the love of God that is in Christ Jesus our Lord."
   (ROMANS 8:39)

"God so loved the world that he gave his one and only Son, that whoever believes in him shall not perish but have eternal life."
     (JOHN 3:16)

"Therefore, if anyone is in Christ, he is a new creation; the old has gone, the new has come!"
     (2 CORINTHIANS 5:17)

"Do not conform any longer to the pattern of this world, but be transformed by the renewing of your mind. Then you will be able to test and approve what God's will is —his good, pleasing and perfect will."
     (ROMANS 12:2)

"If we confess our sins, he is faithful and just and will forgive us our sins and purify us from all unrighteousness."
     (1 JOHN 1:9)

# PRAY

# PRAY

Have you ever been friends with someone who
you never communicated with?

Yeah, me neither.

If you want to know someone, you talk with them. You say things and
they listen. They say things and you listen. It's just how we're wired
to connect with each other.

The same is true when it comes to God. If you want to know God,
you pray to Him. And here's the really great news: Because of Jesus,
you aren't praying to some far-off, mysterious, unknown God. You are
praying to Someone who really understands.

Here's something you might not know:

Before Jesus came to earth, the Israelites connected with God through
priests. The priests would regularly present offerings to God as a
sacrifice to cover over the sins of the people. Once a year on the Day
of Atonement, the high priest would walk through a curtain into a very
holy place in the temple where God's presence dwelled. In that place,
he would make a sacrifice to cover over *all* the sins of the people.

Kind of complicated, I know. But very symbolic. And very powerful.

On the day that Jesus died (actually, in the *moment* Jesus died), the
curtain that separated the most holy place in the temple from the rest
of the world tore open. The separation between God and man was
over. Done. Ended. Finished. Removed. Jesus was the once-and-for-
all sacrifice for sin. And because He paid for our sin, He changed the
way we connect with God from that moment forward.

Just-typing that gets me excited!

**PRAY**

**❂ WHAT ARE YOUR FEARS WHEN IT COMES TO SURRENDERING AND ASKING GOD TO TAKE THE LEAD?**

.......................................................................................

.......................................................................................

.......................................................................................

**❂ WHAT IS ONE AREA OF YOUR LIFE YOU DON'T WANT TO SURRENDER TO GOD? WHY NOT?**

.......................................................................................

.......................................................................................

.......................................................................................

It's natural to feel hesitant. But it's important to know that the payoff is incredible. Being surrendered to God is the best place you can possibly be in life! Why? Because you're inviting the *Creator of the universe* to move on *your* behalf. As a result, you get *His* wisdom, power, purpose, heart, creativity, and peace intersecting with *your* everyday life. When you let God win, you win!

Here's what surrendering to God and His kingdom looks like:

**WHAT GOD WANTS > WHAT I WANT**

Today, pray the following prayer, and then spend some time inviting God to take the lead in specific areas of your life:

*"God, before I pray about **my little kingdoms**, I want to surrender to **Your kingdom**. I want to acknowledge that whatever You want for my life is greater than what I want. I am giving up all of me to all of You. You take the lead."*

# PRAY

## DAY 12

Did you know that one flush of the toilet uses up to four gallons of water? Now, I'm definitely not trying to debate the appropriate circumstances in which one should or should not flush a toilet. That's just a surprising amount of water. I'm talking around 40 gallons of a precious natural resource that you quite literally flush down the toilet each day.

Water is important. I'm sure you've heard a variation of this stat before: you can go *three weeks* without food, but you can only go *three days* without water. Do you find that as strange as I do? Honestly, if I had to choose between a Big Mac and a glass of water, I'm going with the Big Mac every time.

But, like it or not, we're all *dependent* on water. You might even say that water *demands* our *dependence*. We have to drink water. We have no choice.

If you really think about it, we are as dependent on God as we are on water. But He doesn't *demand* our dependence. Instead, He *invites* it.

In Jesus' Sermon on the Mount, He continues The Lord's Prayer with a line about our utter dependence on God:

*"Give us today our daily bread" (Matthew 6:11).*

"Daily bread" is a reference to a time when the Israelites were literally out of food, and God dropped it from the sky every day to keep them alive. *That's* dependence! God says, "Remember when I did that? When you counted on Me to stay alive every day? That's what I want from you right now."

# PRAY

It's okay to ask God for things. In fact, He wants us to do that. But it's important to remember that our asking shouldn't center around what God can do for us—it should center on how much we need Him. Bottom line: **Prayer reminds us that we need God.**

Although there are a lot of ways you and I can practice dependence, I want to start with two simple exercises:

1. **Ask God to help you in areas where you're already doing great.** Does that sound weird? It shouldn't. The truth is, all of our talents and skills come from God. And being dependent means claiming our need for Him in areas where it may not appear as obvious that we need Him.

2. **Write down some things you're thankful for.** Thanksgiving reminds us that good things come from God, not from coincidence or luck. Here are three benefits of being thankful:
   - » Your mood improves.
   - » Your faith in God increases.
   - » Your perspective changes for the better.

Let's practice:

**❂ WRITE DOWN FIVE THINGS YOU'RE THANKFUL FOR, AND THEN SPEND SOME TIME TELLING GOD HOW MUCH YOU NEED HIM:**

1. ................................................................................................................

2. ................................................................................................................

3. ................................................................................................................

4. ................................................................................................................

5. ................................................................................................................

## DAY 13

What creates happiness? Puppies? Laughing babies on YouTube? Getting a date? Getting rich? According to recent research, forgiveness does.

In his article "Forgiveness Is Good for Your Health," Gregg Easterbrook says that people who forgive have better health, less depression, and better social support than those who don't.

In another study, Everett Worthington, Jr. claims that people who don't forgive have stress problems, immune system problems, and heart problems at a higher rate than the population as a whole.

In other words, forgiveness makes you happy, and unforgiveness makes you sick.

Jesus talked about this concept long before psychologists did. Here's what He said:

> *"Forgive us our debts, as we also have forgiven our debtors"* (Matthew 6:12).

Forgiveness is one of those things that I *have* to pray about. When people hurt or offend me, I have to take it to God. And when I talk to God about forgiveness it reminds me of two things:

1. **I need forgiveness.** I do things every day that I know I *shouldn't*. And I neglect to do things that I know I *should*. I think things, do things, and say things that go against what God wants. Yet He continues to offer me grace and forgiveness.

2. **I need to pass on that same forgiveness.** Once we realize how much *we* need forgiveness, it's easier to distribute it to other people. Maybe they don't *deserve* forgiveness. Guess what? Neither do we, yet God still offers it.

It's a simple concept: **God forgave us, so we should forgive others.**

PRAY

But it can be so difficult. And emotional. And powerful. That's why I want you to get in a habit of remembering how God has forgiven you and praying for God to help you forgive others.

**◑ DO YOU HAVE ANY HURT OR ANGER THAT'S CURRENTLY DIRECTED AT SOMEONE? WHAT WAS TAKEN FROM YOU? IN WHAT WAY WERE YOU WRONGED? WHAT ARE YOU OWED?**

.................................................................................................................................

.................................................................................................................................

.................................................................................................................................

**◑ NOW SPEND SOME TIME PRAYING.**

» CONFESS YOUR SINS TO GOD.
» THANK HIM FOR HIS FORGIVENESS.
» FORGIVE THE PEOPLE WHO'VE WRONGED YOU.

# PRAY

## DAY 14

Have you ever had a staring contest with someone? You wait to see which person will be the first to blink. I'm terrible at staring contests because I have exceptionally dry eyes. I blink a lot. I'm blinking right now just thinking about blinking. I bet you're blinking, too.

The average person blinks every four to six seconds. That number is affected by your environment and by how tired you are. But every person on planet earth blinks and blinks often. I guess you could say we blink continually.

In the Bible, Paul tells us to do something else continually. It may surprise you:

*"Pray continually" (1 Thessalonians 5:17).*

Paul didn't really beat around the bush, did he? He was clear about the expectations he had for Jesus-followers. He encourages us to pray and pray often.

I grew up thinking that prayer was reserved for *specific* times and places—before meals and baseball games, during church, before bed, or at night. But here's the cool thing about prayer: **we have access to God—any time, any place.**

Before cell phones were invented, calls could only be made from pay phones or home lines—specific times from specific places. But the reason the profit of the cell phone industry brings in trillions of dollars every year is because it breaks that barrier and allows us to access people any time from virtually any place.

That's what prayer does—it allows you instant access to God. You don't have to wait until church. You don't have to wait until you clean up your act. You don't have to wait until school, work, or practice is over. You can pray to God—**any time, any place.**

# PRAY

If you aren't really sure how to pray continually, here are two suggestions to get you started:

1. **Pray for people.** When you have conversations with people throughout the day, say a quick prayer for them in your mind: *"God, be with Bradley today. Comfort him as he goes through this tough situation with his family."*

2. **Acknowledge and invite.** Before you make it to your next stop—school, practice, rehearsal, work, home, etc.—acknowledge God and invite Him into that place: *"God, before I walk into my house, I want You to know that I need You. Help me to remember You while I'm at home tonight."*

**WHERE ARE SOME PLACES YOU CAN PRACTICE PRAYING CONTINUALLY THIS WEEK? YOUR CAR? THE HALLWAY AT YOUR SCHOOL? YOUR BIOLOGY CLASS?**

........................................................................................................

........................................................................................................

........................................................................................................

# IF YOU WANT TO KNOW GOD . . .
## PRAY TO HIM.

Because of Jesus, you can pray directly to God. Any time. Any place. With boldness. And when you pray, it connects you with God.

There's no magic formula for praying. But there are some things you can keep in mind when you're talking to God.

## Pray by honoring God.

## Pray with humility.

## Pray with gratitude.

## Pray with honesty.

## Pray for forgiveness.

*"Do not be anxious about anything, but in everything, by prayer and petition, with thanksgiving, present your requests to God" (Philippians 4:6).*

# TALK

# TALK

Here are two things I know about you: You like to talk about things you like. You like to hang out with people who talk about things you like.

Isn't that true?

Whether it's video games, boys, movies, UFC, breakdancing, lacrosse, guitar amps, or robots, we all have stuff we like to talk about.

Name one thing you like to talk about:

Name one person you like to talk about it with:

When you talk to                                            about

                              , you probably both discover more about it.

Peter and John were two people who liked to talk about Jesus.

Maybe that seems strange to you. But these were two guys who hung out with Jesus. In fact, they were in Jesus' inner circle. They knew Him well. And because they knew Jesus—saw what He did and heard what He said—they talked about Him like crazy.

In fact, the book of Acts records an interesting story when Peter and John got in trouble for running their mouths about Jesus. They were standing outside the temple saying stuff like this:

> *"Salvation is found in no one else, for there is no other name under heaven given to men by which we must be saved"* (Acts 4:12).

That's pretty cool, right? Not if you were a religious leader from back in the day. They still weren't convinced that Jesus was God's Son. So they threw Peter and John in jail for the night. The next day the religious leaders told Peter and John they were free to go, as long as they promised to stop talking about Jesus.

Okay, that's not a good idea. Listen to what Jesus says:

*"You are the light of the world. A city on a hill cannot be hidden" (Matthew 5:14).*

Do you know someone whose world seems a little dark right now? Maybe you know someone who's making terrible decisions. Or maybe you know someone who's intelligent or good with words, but when it comes to faith they're just . . . well, in the dark. That's what Jesus was referring to—a world full of darkness.

Into that world, Jesus sends *you*. In a world where the power's out, you have a flashlight. Not because you're perfect, you have it all together, or you're better than anyone. But because you've met Jesus—which means you've met the Inventor of light.

So, use your influence to shine a light. Sometimes that means *talking*. And sometimes that means *doing*. But the key is this: God wants to use you. **You were created to be a light in the dark.**

 **START WITH ONE PERSON WHO NEEDS "LIGHT" IN THEIR LIFE RIGHT NOW. WRITE DOWN THEIR NAME. PRAY FOR THEM. PRAY THEY SEE THE LIGHT OF JESUS IN YOU. ASK GOD FOR OPPORTUNITIES TO TALK TO THEM, OR TO SIMPLY BE A LIGHT FOR THEM.**

......................................................................................................................

......................................................................................................................

......................................................................................................................

......................................................................................................................

......................................................................................................................

......................................................................................................................

# IF YOU WANT TO KNOW GOD . . .
## TALK ABOUT HIM WITH YOUR FRIENDS.

Before you talk to other people about God, it might help for you to take some time to think about what God has done in your life. What is your story? How has God shown up in your life to reveal who He is and how much He loves you?

**↻ WRITE YOUR STORY—THE STORY OF THE WAYS GOD HAS SHOWN UP IN YOUR LIFE—HERE:**

When and how did you first believe God's story?

How has God changed your life?

How has God answered prayers for you?

What has God taught you?

And you know what? These questions could be great to *talk* about with some other people who know God. Ask them about their stories. You never know what you might learn about God when you **talk about Him with your friends**.

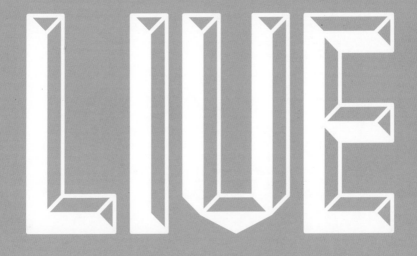

# LIVE

Think of someone who's done a lot for you. Maybe they've given up things for you, provided for you, loved you. You know you can never completely pay them back. But don't you wish you could do *something*?

Now think about this: Has God done more for you, or have you done more for God? (I'm pretty sure we both know that answer, so you don't have to write it down.)

Paul, who wrote the book of Romans, talks a little bit about this. In Romans 11:35-36, he basically says you were made for God.

> *Or who has given a gift to him that he might be repaid? For from him and through him and to him are all things. To him be glory forever. Amen. (Romans 11:35-36).*

Get it? You were made for God.

That's a big thought. It means that everything about you is designed to respond to Him. You were created so that you could reflect God to the world around you. You were made to make Him known.

Don't believe me?

Think about this: There's something inside all of us that wants to worship. We have a desire to celebrate something. Most of us are good at getting so wrapped up in something that everyone around us sees our enthusiasm. In fact, our excitement gets others enthusiastic, too.

Maybe you have felt this way about a movie, football team, new band, crush, more-than-crush, school dance, or an item on the 99-cent menu at Wendy's.

But here's what Paul tells us: If you already have the urge to worship—get over-the-top excited about something, wrapped up in it, and fired up to celebrate it—**why not worship the most important thing**, the thing you were created to worship? Why not worship Jesus?

**LIVE**

◑ **HERE ARE A FEW WAYS TO WORK WITH ALL YOUR HEART:**

» Work hard. Show up on time, prepared to give your best effort. If you're in the marching band, play the tuba like God Himself is sitting in the bleachers at halftime. If you run cross-country, run like you're running toward God's big pearly gates. (If you're anything like me, you don't have to run very far to feel like you might meet God at any moment.) If you work at Moe's, wrap that burrito like Jesus is staring at you through the glass.

» Have a good attitude. When bosses, teachers, parents, coaches, and directors can say about Christian students, "They have a great attitude," that's an awesome representation of God.

» Be smart. You don't have to be the best at everything you do, but you can always be competent. Be informed. Learn everything you can.

» Pay attention. Care about other people on your team, in your band, or at your job. Ask them questions. Listen to their answers. It's a huge opportunity for influence.

When you work in such a way that makes other people notice—and you do it *because* you represent Jesus—it points people towards the awesome God whom you follow.

◑ **WRITE DOWN A COUPLE AREAS WHERE YOU COULD WORK HARDER.**

........................................................................................................

........................................................................................................

........................................................................................................

*Today, work at whatever you do with more passion. Consider it an act of worship. Ask God to help you represent Him well in everything you do.*

# LIVE

## DAY 27

The world's most expensive bed is called the *Baldacchino Supreme*. It was created by Stuart Hughes. One of its special features is 236 pounds of 24-karat gold. The cost? Well over $6 million dollars.

Now, if I sleep on a bed that cost $6 million, I better wake up with no acne and better muscle definition!

People are willing to put a high price tag on rest—probably because it's hard to come by these days. People are busy. In a survey of 882 students, 90 percent said they felt stressed because they were too busy.

I realize some of you may be thinking, *"I wish I had too much going on . . . I wish I had anything going on. I'm just so bored!"* If you're in the 10 percent that doesn't feel too busy, today will still apply to you.

The writer of Psalm 46 talks about worshiping God because He protects us and takes care of us. Within that, he addresses the idea of rest:

> *"Be still, and know that I am God; I will be exalted among the nations, I will be exalted in the earth" (Psalm 46:10).*

Here are three reasons you should rest:

1. **God can handle your worries.** God is a big God who can handle *all* your stuff. He cares deeply about your life. His ability to handle your worry is different than your ability to handle it. When you invite Him to get involved in all the things that stress you out, He brings His power, plans, purpose, and ability into your world.

2. **Rest makes space for God.** Rest is not about laziness or doing nothing. It's about allowing room in your heart, mind, life, and schedule for your relationship with God. You can worship God and enjoy Him more when you slow down and appreciate Him.

**3. You'll work better.** You see this in other areas of your life. For all of you fitness freaks who work out constantly, you probably know that your muscles grow when you rest. It's the same in your life—you will be *more effective* in school, work, relationships (the list goes on and on) when you rest.

Bottom line, **when you trust God, you will rest.** You can accept the fact that God is in control, and purposely creates space to worship Him as you let your minds and bodies recover.

◐ **WRITE DOWN SOME OF THE BIG PIECES OF YOUR SCHEDULE TODAY (OR TOMORROW IF IT'S LATE). CIRCLE THE PART OF THE DAY WHERE YOU'RE GOING TO WORSHIP THROUGH REST:**

...........................................................................................................

...........................................................................................................

...........................................................................................................

...........................................................................................................

...........................................................................................................

...........................................................................................................

...........................................................................................................

...........................................................................................................

...........................................................................................................

...........................................................................................................

...........................................................................................................

Asa Candler, an early president of Coca-Cola, was worried that other companies would steal Coke's recipe. He insisted that no one ever write it down, and he shredded all documents that could possibly reveal its ingredients.

Today, only two people alive know the formula, and the list of ingredients is locked in a bank vault.

Coca-Cola realized something significant:
- » We have a recipe.
- » It's awesome.
- » We must hide it.

Jesus also realized something significant:
- » We have a recipe.
- » It's awesome.
- » We must NOT hide it.

When asked what was the greatest commandment in the Law, Jesus replied:

> *"'Love the Lord your God with all your heart and with all your soul and with all your mind.' This is the first and greatest commandment. And the second is like it: 'Love your neighbor as yourself'" (Matthew 22:37-39).*

There's the secret recipe: *love God and love others*. It's the way to know God, and it's the way to make God known. In the same way that Coca-Cola's secret recipe makes them stand out, *love is what makes Jesus-followers different from the rest of the world.*

God is big and vast. He's infinite. There is so much you can learn about Him. But as you approach Him, **start with love.**

# LIVE

The Bible is full of incredible insights, narratives, and challenges. It is so relevant, but at times complicated. I hope you study it and are changed by it. But I hope you **start with love.**

We've talked about a lot of things you can do in this journal—read and memorize Scripture, pray, live in community, talk with unbelievers, worship, work hard, and rest. But I hope you always **start with love.**

And not just in what you *think* or in what you *feel*—in what you *do*. **Everything we *do* should be done through the filter of love**—it is our secret formula.

As we close, I'd love to pray for you:

God, thank You for each student who has gone through this journal. I ask that You continually show them Your love. Remind them that You are love, and that Your love never fails. Show them how to love You, Father, and teach them how to love others. In Jesus' name I ask these things, amen.

---

AND AS YOU CONTINUE YOUR QUEST TO KNOW GOD,
## START WITH LOVE

---

| When you | When you | When you | When you |
|---|---|---|---|
| **HEAR** | **PRAY** | **TALK** | **LIVE** |
| Read the Bible through the filter of love. | Pray that God will show you how to love Him and others. | Let your conversations with believers and unbelievers be founded in love. | Let your worship be a response to God's love. |

## WORSHIP CAN BE PRETTY PERSONAL.

» Some people like to worship God by singing loudly to God with their arms up in the air. Other people prefer to worship God by being very quiet.

» Some people like to worship God with lots of other people. Others prefer to worship God by walking alone outside.

» Some people like to dance, play an instrument, or use a talent to worship God. Others like to worship God by giving money or stuff to people who can benefit from it, or by using their time and energy to serve others.

There are a lot of ways to honor God with your worship.